CRICUT

Design Space For Beginners

The Simple Step By Step Guide On How To Start To Do Extraordinary Cricut Projects

TABLE OF CONTENTS

INTRODUCTION

Cricut has amazing capabilities that will enhance your creativity either as a beginner or a professional. As a matter of fact, this machine can make you come off as a master designer even if you aren't so creative in real life.

Finding a tool or companion that gives you freedom to explore your passion is a great way to be a professional crafter. Thankfully, for anyone who wishes to go into crafting, Cricut has made an amazing machine with advance cutting technology that will help you cut, design, and bring all your beautiful craft ideas to life.

It is important to know what tools and accessories to use with your Cricut to cut down on your preparation time and save yourself a lot of headaches! The Circuit machine is very versatile and can be used with many types of materials to assemble any time of project you can think up.

In this book, you will learn all there is to know about what your Cricut machine can do and how to get the most from your machine. We'll reveal all the trade secrets that will have you using your machine like a professional in no time flat!

My aim in writing this cricut manual is that by the time you are done reading, you become a complete pro with the cricut machine, and also that you start executing your own projects right away.

Enjoy reading!

CHAPTER 1:

UNDERSTANDING CRICUT

What is a Cricut Machine?

The cricut maker machine is an electronic die-cutter for different materials including papers, vinyl and fabrics into desired shapes and patterns. This machine is capable of awesome design cuts and markings on a large variety of materials and very easy to use.

The cricut machines have the capability to cut large number of materials accurately and quickly. The range of materials varies from the delicate paper to leather then to thicker materials such as wood. With the aid of powerful rotary blades, the machine glides and rolls over any fabrics effortlessly leaving smooth and accurate cut on the material.

Cricut machines, at the core, are really cool printers.

Technically, they die cutters and creative planners that help you put together cool designs for various items that you want to make. There are a lot of models out there, and many great types to choose from.

The Explore series of machines contain software called Cricut Design Space, which allows for you to design in the space whatever you want to make, and then literally print it out.

If you're sick and tired of making the same images each time, or you're looking to cut out a design in vinyl without tearing your hair out, then a Cricut machine could really help you.

The Cricut is a die-cutting machine, which is also known as a craft plotter or a cutting machine. Its format allows you to do projects that range from simple to complex on a seemingly limitless number of materials. From thin metal sheets to fabric, you can bring your designs to life with this innovative craft machine.

Cricut has a massive base of users who are enthusiastic to share their projects, tutorials, tips for care, tricks for usage, and other materials that can be used with their Cricut Makers. The resources for a crafter using a Cricut machine are nearly limitless.

A Cricut machine has the capacity to cut materials ranging from paper to faux leather, just to mention a few. In case you don't have good handwriting, you can also use this machine to that effect. In other words, you can make a Cricut do the job of a printer for you.

This is possible loading a marker in the accessory slot of the machine. When you do this, you can then proceed by making the machine draw the design you desire. Hence, the Cricut machine is also a multifaceted machine that is designed to bring some versatility to your table.

Designs written by loading the marker of the

accessory slot of the Cricut machine are always exquisite. Interestingly, you don't have to even use physical cartridges with some versions of the Cricut machine! The Explore series is a typical example of such versions of Cricut machines.

These series of Cricut machines are designed such that you can use the online design software instead. What this implies is that any shape or text you desire can be selected from this platform. The specific design you want can then be sent to the machine in order for you to cut it out.

Interestingly, the Explore series of the Cricut machine also makes it possible for direct upload. Hence, you can simply upload the particular design you want and use the machine to cut it out.

In addition to this awesomeness, a digital sewing pattern library is stored in the cricut maker for the user to access hundreds of patterns from different brand names such as Riley Blake and Simplicity. You can pick a number of projects from the library and boom, the machine cuts every piece you desire.

The Cricut Design Space allows the user to access any one of the over 50 projects in its library including 25 digital sewing patterns. Not only that, it also allows you to upload an image to create a customized design of your own. The capabilities of the Cricut Maker Machine are just endless: Iron-on decorations on t-shirts, leather, vinyl decors, wood puzzles and sewing projects are some of the DIY or craft projects you can do using the machine.

The Cricut Design Space software can be operated with IOS or Android device having a USB charging.

How Does It Work?

When you see the finished product from a Cricut machine, you will definitely be blown away. The neatness and appealing look of a typical project done with the Cricut machine will take your breath away. However, only a few people understand the process involved in the creation of such amazing designs.

Curious to know how the Cricut machine is able to cut out materials effectively? You are reading the right book. There are three major steps involved when using the Cricut machine:

Have a Design

If you have a PC, you can access the Cricut Design Space to access the library of designs. If you have a Mac, you can access the same platform to select a huge variety of designs. In case you don't have any of these two but possesses an iPhone or iPad, you can use the Design Space for iOS.

If what you have is an android, you are covered as well. This is because you can take advantage of the Design Space for Android. These are online platforms where you can select any design that best suits your taste.

You can also customize a ready-made design to suit your need. For example, you can resize it or modify the shape. You can also add a text or image as you wish till you have the design just as you want it.

Prepare the Machine

Having selected the design, you intend cutting out with the machine, you are ready for the next step. The machine needs to be prepared by turning it on. Once you switch on the machine, you actually don't need to do anything.

You don't have to press any button unless you are using the machine for the first time. In that case, the machine will give you instructions on what to do. It is that simple.

That is why both beginners and experts can make use of the Cricut machine without issues. Your computer or phone will have to be paired with the machine via Bluetooth for the first time. However, this will not be needed subsequently because the machine will remember the pairing.

Hence, once the machine is switched on, the pairing between the phone and the machine becomes automatic. The implication of this is that once the machine is switched on, the machine is ready. The next step is to send the design to the machine.

Send the Design to the Machine

This is the last stage of the process of cutting with the Cricut machine. Once the machine is powered on, at the top right corner of the screen, you will see the Make It button. This button is a big green button on the Cricut Design Space.

The first thing the software does is to preview the various mats you have. A mat represents a sheet of material; hence, having two different colors in your project implies two mats. There are times that your project can be a combination of a fabric and a paper.

During such occurrences, you will have a mat

representing each material utilized for the project. Once you have prepared the machine, you need to decide the dimension with which the machine will do the cutting. If you intend making two cards, the machine has to be instructed to make two project copies.

You will find this option at the top left of the Cricut Design Space. Most of the materials you will be cutting will be cut at 12″ × 12″ size. This is because this is the standard size that is the most prominent on the Cricut machine.

However, if you prefer a different dimension, you can always alter it. The mirror switch has to be flipped to mirror the design you want in case you want an iron-on design. This has to be done to guarantee that the alteration is reflected by the finished project.

Once you are set to send the design to the Cricut, you will click Continue. This option can be seen at the bottom right corner of the Cricut Design Space. It is easy to continue at this point because the software will prompt you to take you through what ought to be done.

Don't get what up about how to set up different projects of different materials and colors. This is because the instructions you need will be displayed on the screen, and you can easily follow through. Once you follow the instructions presented to you by the machine, you are guaranteed of top-quality cuttings.

The machine will request that you pick the particular material you want to use for the first mat. Simply choose whether it is paper, vinyl, fabric, leather, or any other material. Once you do this, the machine will automatically adjust pressure, speed, and the brush blade as necessary.

Hence, just ensure you do your part of instructing the machine to do your bidding as desired. You can trust the Cricut machine from that point to do all that is needed for a perfect project. After the machine has adjusted itself to cut, you will put the material into the Cricut cutting mat.

At this point, you will then load the machine with the mat. What if I am using different materials for my project? That is also not an issue worth disturbing yourself about.

This is because the software will take you through how to go about loading different materials. Once you are done loading the machine with the mat containing the material, you are good to go. This is because you will be prompted by the machine concerning setting the dial cutting, drawing, or scoring.

The machine will proceed to cut out the mat. The pieces that have been cut out can then be gathered by you and used as desired. This is how the Cricut machine works, and it is basically the same principle for every project.

It is obvious that you don't have to be a genius before you are qualified to use the machine. The instructions are simplified such that anyone who can understand basic English language can use it. Therefore, if you have been thinking that you might not be able to operate this machine, you are wrong.

What Can the Cricut Do?

When you break it down to its most basic operation, the Cricut does two things. It cuts, and it draws. These two functions, however, have over a million uses and can be used on hundreds of materials, making it a truly versatile crafting powerhouse. Breaking it down to these two features seems almost like an injustice to the adaptability and versatility that this machine truly has.

If you like to make ornaments during the holiday season, the Cricut can help you make vinyl decals for that. If you like to make ornate greeting cards for every occasion, the Cricut can cut, emboss, score, and engrave accents for any design you can dream up in the Cricut Design Space. If you like making hats and t-shirts for group and family activities, Cricut has a whole range of iron-on materials that can be used for those!

Personalize everything you can imagine and more with Cricut products that are meant specifically to help you and crafters all over the world express themselves! There will be no project that can't be made better with a stencil, decal, sticker, or accent created or augmented with the Cricut and its host of customization features!

The Cricut Design Space library contains drawings of different colors with which you can use to cut materials or you can decide to input your own image and drawings using Photoshop, your tablet or Illustrator. You can also draw a hand sketch, scan it into your machine to draw and cut for you.

There are more than 50 crafts you can do using your Cricut Maker machine. Here, I will discuss in simple terms these amazing items:

- **Cut fabrics:** the rotary blade was designed to cut seamlessly through any fabric including silk, denim, chiffon, and heavy canvass. Coupled with the mat, hundreds of fabrics can be cut without any backing. This is amazing!

- **Vinyl Decals and stickers:** Is cutting vinyl decals and stickers your hobby, then you need Cricut Maker machine as your companion. Get the design inputted in the Design Space Software and instruct the machine to cut. As easy as that. The delivery will be wonderful. So what are you waiting for? Get to work!

- **Greeting Cards:** The power and precision of the Cricut Maker makes cutting of paper as well as making greeting cards craft less tedious and saves ample time. Your Christmas cards, birthday cards, success cards and other greeting cards will be delivered with accurate, unique and amazing style.

- **Quilts**: There are arrays of quilting pattern in the sewing pattern library of the Cricut Maker machine thanks to Cricut teaming up with Riley Blake Designs. With this library, you can cut and join quilt pieces accurately and sew them together using the Cricut Maker machine. The quilt designs are amazing.

- **T-shits:** Cutting heat transfer vinyl to be transferred on fabrics is a job the Cricut Maker does so well. First design on the Design Space and load into the Cricut Maker. Instruct the Maker to start cutting the heat transfer vinyl. After cutting, you then iron the transfer onto your T-shirt.

- **Cuts Balsa Wood:** It was stated previously that the Cricut Maker can cut through materials up to 2.4mm with pressure up to 4kg. Cutting wood up to this thickness can be done seamlessly using the Knife Blade that comes with the Cricut Maker. This is amazing.

- **Sewing patterns:** There are hundreds of sewing patterns which you can access once you buy the Cricut maker Machine. Patterns from Riley Blake Designs and Simplicity are included. All you need do is select any of the designs and the Cricut Maker will do the cutting for you.

- **Holiday decorations:** The rotary blade of the Cricut Maker can cut through fabrics of different types. This is a big plus to crafters assigned with decorations for holiday programmes like the birthday, wedding, anniversary and Christmas celebrations. Let the Cricut Maker do the cutting for you while you do the joining and fixing.

- **Dolls and Toys:** The sewing pattern library still comes to play here. Select the type of design and let the Cricut Maker cut the material for you. Kids love Dolls and toys. Do not deny them this wonderful experience of homemade dolls and toys.

- **Baby Clothes:** You can design that old children's clothes to become new again by being creative or even the ones you just bought from the store.

Cricut subscription

Cricut Access is the software that gives you access to images, fonts, and the like. You will need to purchase this if you plan on using your Cricut machine, period, and if you don't have the software already, I suggest purchasing it.

The monthly option is perfect for beginners and offers over 400 different fonts and 90,000 different images. And it comes with a 10% savings on any additional Cricut purchases you need, as well as a 10% savings on premium images and fonts, such as Disney fonts. You'll also have access to a priority member line.

The next membership option is annual, which is exactly the same as the basic, but you don't have to pay as much – just $7.99 per month, upfront. It's good if you're serious about getting into Cricut.

Finally, you have the premium option, which is the same price as monthly and offers unlimited access to the same fonts and images, savings on both products and licenses, and a 50% extra savings on licensed images and fonts, along with some ready-to-make projects. If you spend over $50 on the Cricut store, you earn free shipping. Personally, I think this is the best option if you plan on spending a lot of money on Cricut items, and you're in it for the long haul. However, if you're just beginning, the monthly membership is probably a better choice, because you can cancel this at any time.

Membership allows you to save a little bit on premium ideas and licensed designs – the more you make with your Cricut machine, the more you save, and you'll realize that you could save a lot really fast. On average, customers say that they make up the subscription costs with the money they save, and the coolest thing is that there is so much to choose from, you can find some beautiful designs. It is definitely great if you want exclusive content.

Craft Stores

If you are someone who enjoys going to a store to purchase items for a project over ordering them online, you too have many options to purchase your materials from. Craft stores have been around for a long time, but they have just recently started providing materials for all the Cricut Machines. You can easily think of a project and run to your nearest craft store and get everything you need to get started on your project that day. This also comes in handy if you are missing something you thought you had, or run out of something you need right away. These stores are always in convenient locations and making material gathering easy for everyone!

Cricut Website

Cricut online provides a great resource for buying materials for your Cricut projects. They keep their products up to date and often offer products that are created by designers. This is a great option for materials that are unlike what is sold in-store and online. Another great perk of buying directly from Cricut is that if you are a Design Space member, you will receive 10% off every purchase you make through them. Cricut takes care of their customers in more ways than one!

CHAPTER 2:

CRICUT MODELS

There are four main types of Cricut machines, all of which are used to cut out various designs.

Cricut Explore Air

It functions almost similar to Cricut Explore Air 2. The only difference is that this machine cuts a bit slower. As compared to Cricut Explore Air 2, and the project thus takes time to finish.

This machine is different from the Cricut Explore One in two ways. First, it has a Bluetooth-enable device and therefore does not require cable for connection between your device and the machine. Secondly, you can score, write and cut at the same time due to the double tool holder. These two features make the Cricut Explore Air more expensive than the Cricut Explore One.

The machine was designed for the user to have an easy to understand experience while using it. With the Bluetooth enabled device, you can send designs directly from another Bluetooth enable device including your phone.

Cricut Explore 1

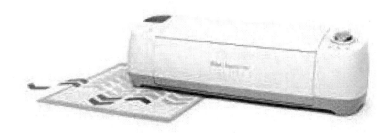

It is the first ever Cricut Machine that eliminated the need to use cartridges and introduced the internet Design Space feature allowing you to make designs and projects of your choice. The drawback that it has is that it does not have a Bluetooth, so you need to attach a computer directly to it. Otherwise, it would not work. It's pretty basic, but for under $200, you're getting a great machine to start with. This is the best for beginners, since you can cut precisely, score, write, and do a lot more with it, and you don't need to use cartridges. Again, this is not really a problem, especially if you're someone who uses your machine a lot. This also isn't wireless, but if you won't be using your computer or iPad in another room, this isn't an issue.

It isn't a double tool cartridge, either, so you won't be able to score and cut at the same time, but it can be done separately. However, this isn't a problem unless you have to do both.

This is the most affordable machine of the Cricut

with more than 50000 images accompanying it. The images allow users to have flexibility in the choice of design and good insight into the capability of the machine. It is designed using advanced technology for precise cutting, scoring and writing capabilities of the Cricut Explore Air Machine lines. A smart dial setting attached to the Cricut Explore One eliminates the use of manual setting.

Cricut Explore One does not come with any Bluetooth enabled device; therefore, a cable is required to connect between your Cricut and your device or a Bluetooth adapter using the USB port that comes with the machine.

Another challenge of this Cricut machine is that there is no double tool cartridge to score and cut during the same pass, therefore, the need to score and cut separately. Other disadvantages of this machine is that Design Space software can only be accessed online and only cut light materials. The challenge of this machine comes into play when you have a lot of work to do involving scoring and cutting.

Cricut Explore Air 2

Cricut Explore Air 2 is a diminution to the Cricut Maker. Although it is not compatible with the knife blade or rotary cutter, it can still cut hundreds of materials. It is better in a way that it cuts things twice faster than a Cricut Explore Air does. It is also cheaper than the Cricut maker, usually less than half of the price.

If you like pastel colors, this might be one to consider – but again, the price could be a little hefty for those just starting out with Cricut machines. This machine is different from the Cricut Explore Air in two ways also. First, it is bigger than Cricut Explore Air and secondly, it is two times faster in cutting and writing than the Cricut Explore Air. It is more expensive than Cricut Explore Air obviously and saves ample time for job delivery. It is also designed for easy to understand experience of the user.

The speed at which this machine performs the cutting and writing operation is its main selling point. It has both normal and fast modes of operation. The Cricut Explore Air 2 comes in nice green color and very beautiful too. Added to these advantages is the powerful cutting blades, easy storage compartments, and over 3000 project already made for users to explore and used to their satisfaction.

The Cricut Maker

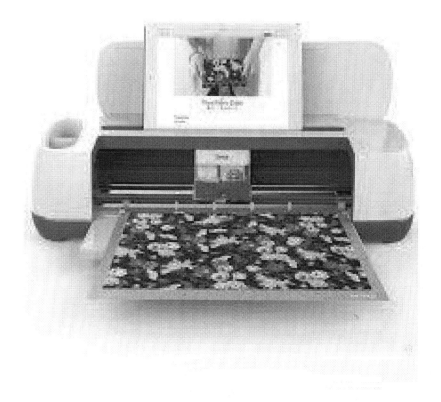

The Cricut Maker is the latest and most advanced of Cricut's cutting machines. It is similar in design to the Cricut Explore types and performs the same function except that new and advanced features were added to enhance its capabilities. For example, the Cricut Maker uses tiny rotary blade to cut unbounded fabrics which eliminates the use of stabilizers used in the Cricut Explore line. Cricut Maker cuts and writes on the materials placed on its adhesive mat. This machine is designed to help users make amazing sewing and DIY projects. Like the Cricut Explore Air 2, it has a wireless enable device; it is compact and dependable too.

The Cricut Maker is the only machine which has a rotary cutter for fabrics and crepe paper. To cut thick materials like wood, foam board, etc, Cricut maker has now a knife blade installed in it which makes the wood cutting easier and better. The rotary cutter comes along with the packing of Cricut maker. But you will have to buy the knife blade separately. If you wish to change or switch different cutting tools, then you have to undo the clamp on side "B." After you have opened the clamp, put the tool of your choice and then close it. All this tells about how Cricut maker is recently the best and extremely convenient to use. You can cut unbonded fabric with this, so you won't need to buy a stabilizer or a tiny rotary blade. It can also cut thicker materials, even balsa wood or thicker leather, and it can score items with a scoring wheel. This system is used with a variety of tools, which we'll get into. It is the priciest option at $399, but for that price, you'll be able to do a whole lot with it.

The capabilities of the Cricut Maker include cutting thicker materials up to 2.4mm thickness using Knife Blade, cut fabrics of the size 12 x 24 inches and 11.5 inches wide, the Scoring Wheel to score all sorts of materials for razor-sharp creases and folds, and its adaptive tool system for cutting hundreds of materials. The capability of the Cricut Maker Machine is far from been exhausted because more tools for its adaptive tool systems are been tested by Cricut and due for release any moment.

This machine has a rotary blade for cutting tough fabrics. By its gliding and rolling actions, this special tool is empowered to cut through tough fabrics like a sharp knife. This tool is incredible in the way it gets job done compared to other Cricut machines, it is just amazing. These two blades (rotary and knife) makes the Cricut Maker a unique desktop cutter with cutting pressure of 4kg.

Note that the smallest size Cricut recommends for cutting is ¾" using rotary blade and fabric mat.

The disadvantages of the Cricut Maker include a limited cutting space and the Design Space software is web-based. These limitations do not in any way change the fact that Cricut Maker is the king among the Cricut cutter line.

What is the best Cricut Machine to buy as a beginner?

This is definitely the most important thing that comes to your mind while you learn everything about the Cricut Machine.

Buying the best Cricut machine would complement

your creativity and would help you create crafts, designs, projects, and ornaments. First off, you need to know about buying Cricut machines is that all Cricut Machines work in the same manner.

The thing that sets them apart or creates a difference in Cricut machine is the unique features that are designated to them. The similarity that every Cricut machine has is that each machine uses a free software called Design Space. It is important to know that every cutting machine has its own software which is difficult to learn.

With that being said, if you are looking for a Cricut machine at a reasonable price, then I would recommend you to buy Cricut Explore Air 2. It would also be easy to use if you are a beginner. But if you have enough budget, then Cricut maker would definitely be the best option.

CHAPTER 3:

MATERIALS THAT CAN BE WORKED ON USING CRICUT MACHINE

Most people believe that they can only cut paper and vinyl with the Cricut machine. You will soon find once you get started using your machine that it can actually cut different types of materials! In this section, we will go over a variety of them in detail to get a better understanding of how truly remarkable the Cricut machine really is! Get inspired by a collection of diverse, high-quality materials, all designed to cut perfectly with Cricut machines. Material finishes ranging from fun and flashy, to polished and rich. These materials make it easy to achieve exactly the look you are after. Once you get more comfortable using all the different types of materials, you will easily be able to create projects that have multiple materials in one! Utilize resources such as this book to refer to when you have questions relating to what type of material to use and when. The more you know, the better your project will be!

Vinyl

Adhesive vinyl for Cricut cutting machines come in a wide variety of colors, designs, and uses. The adhesive properties can either be semi-permanent (easily removable with adhesive remover) or permanent. Semi-permanent is typically used for projects indoors; such as wall decals or window clings. Permanent vinyl would be used for outdoor use, such as holiday décor and tabletop designs. Those are perfect for making stickers and indoor and outdoor items, and even "printing" on mugs and T-shirts! Once you get into it, it's truly addictive to acquire different colors and types. For example, you can get chalkboard vinyl, which is awesome for labeling, or outdoor vinyl, which will look great on your car window. These materials can be purchased at virtually any craft shop, and they aren't too expensive if you do a little canvassing. Double check that it is indeed the type of vinyl you are looking for, though.

Vinyl is the most commonly used material for Cricut projects outside of paper because it is one of the most versatile materials to work with. Adhesive vinyl is a great starting point for creators who are new to Cricut but want to branch out outside of paper crafting. Adhesive vinyl is a material that will need to be weeded, as designs are typically cut out of the vinyl and the negative space will need to be removed in order to see the design.

Paper

There is a wide variety of paper products that can be cut using the Cricut machine. Some varieties include cardstock, which is one of the most popular, corrugated cardboard, foil embossed, Kraft board, scrapbooking paper, pearl, sparkle/shimmer, and poster board. Paper products can come in a wide range of sizes, with 12"x12" being the most common and easily applied type as it fits perfectly on a 12"x12" cutting mat. Paper is most commonly used in card projects, but it can also assist in wall décor, gift boxes, cake toppers, lantern projects. Most crafters familiar with the Cricut recommend starting with the paper project first, to get a handle of the different options Cricut cutters to have. Paper allows you to create intricate designs and get familiar with cutting blade depth at the same time. What you have to remember is that you need something to practice on, and a cheap printer paper works wonderfully for that. You won't feel bad for making mistakes because the material does not cost much. If you are feeling more creative than usual, you may get the colored paper too. This way, when you get the hang of cutting, you can create letters for cars or stencils.

The following materials can only be used with the Cricut Maker machine.

Chipboard

The Cricut website sells a variety pack of this type of material, which is great for getting to know the material and what projects to use it effectively. It is suggested for use on projects such as sturdy wall art, school projects, photo frames and more. Since this material has a 1.5mm thickness, it can only be cut using the Cricut Knife blade. Chipboard is great for any time of project that requires dimensions such as gingerbread or haunted house around the holidays!

Fabric

The fabric is great if you have the Cricut Maker. Chances are that you will want to cut some textile with this machine on hand; that's why you should stock up on that and get extra just in case. You can obtain some cheap, scrappy fabrics to practice on before moving on to the proper fabrics for the projects.

This simple yet classic material is another favorite

among Cricut Maker users. Many use fabrics to create custom clothing, home décor, and wall art. Imagine all the times you went out looking for the perfect top or skirt only to come back home empty handed after many hours of searching. It would be ideal to find exactly what you want when you want it! Now, without the help of a bulky and outdated sewing machine, you can make simple and affordable clothing exactly the look and feel you want! Fabric is also a great material to make homemade gifts for friends and family. Lots of people enjoy curling up on the couch during the winter months with a cozy quilt and a favorite movie.

Felt

Blended fibers between natural and synthetic are also common among craft felts. Felt is commonly used to help young children distinguish among different types of textiles. Felt is also commonly used in craft projects for all ages. The felt is easily cut with your Cricut Machine, no Deep Cut blade required! Felt can be used for fun décor, kid's crafts, baby toys, stuffed shapes and more! When starting out on the Cricut Maker, this is one of the best materials to start out with. This material is very forgiving and will allow you to keep the gift-giving spirit going! This material is also great for creating faux flowers. You can bring the outside in, without the maintenance or worrying about children or pets getting into a mess!

Cardstock

If you plan on making cards or labels, cardstock is a must. The more, the better. It's really awesome to have a large pile of it and just be able to cut to your heart's content. It will also help practicing on once you have perfected cutting normal printing paper.

Fondant

Fondant is for those bakers out there. There is a possibility that you already have extra fondant lazing about in your home. However, it never hurts to have more. The awesome thing about fondant is that you can reuse it to an extent, depending on how well it freezes or how big the need is to freeze it before cutting. Of course, it is useful to have back up materials for the days that you are in a crafty sort of mood. Most materials are available on the Cricut website so you can order them along with your Cricut machine. Everything will be delivered at once, and you won't have to buy anything again for a while.

It also depends on what sort of material you will be interested in creating something awesome with. If you are going to cut wood, for instance, you will have to stock up on that as you will be going through it quite fast if you are an enthusiastic and excitable crafter.

CHAPTER 4:

TOOLS AND ACCESSORIES OF CRICUT

Cricut has much to offer in the way of tools and accessories. There are machines they offer to suit different crafting purposes, which have their own accessories and tools as well.

For the Cricut cutting machines, here is what's available:

Cricut Maker Cutting Blades

In addition to the Explore Cutting blade, the Cricut Maker has additional cutting blades that allow for intricate cutting details on a variety of materials.

The Cricut Maker comes with one additional blade, the revolutionary rotary cutting blade for use on cutting all sorts of fabrics. Unlike the average rotary blade, this one lasts far longer because it avoids the nicks that typically come with its line of duty. You can buy additional blades individually, but one blade should last throughout multiple projects.

Cutting Mats

Cricut cutting mats come in a variety of sizes and degree of stickiness. Depending on what material you are using, you will want less or more stickiness on your mat, to hold the material in place while cutting.

The Circuit Weeder

The weeder tool, which looks similar to a dental pick, is used for removing negative space from a vinyl project. This weeder tool is a **must** when doing any type of project that involves vinyl. Trying to get rid of access vinyl is nearly impossible without a weeder especially with materials like glitter iron-on. A weeder is a useful tool for any type of project using adhesives. Instead of picking up the adhesive with your fingertips, user the weeder tool and keep your fingers sticky mess free!

The Cricut Scraper

The Circuit Scraper tool is essential (and a lifesaver!) when you need to rid your cutting mat of excess negative bits. This tool typically works best with paper, such as cardstock, but other materials can easily be scraped up as well. Use the flexibility of the mat to your advantage as you scrap the bits off the mat, to ensure you are not scraping up the adhesive on the mat as well. You can also use the Cricut Scraper as a score line holder, which allows you to fold over the score-line with a nice crisp edge. It can also be used as a burnishing tool for Cricut transfer tape, as it will allow seamless separation of the transfer tape from the backing.

The Cricut Spatula

A spatula is a must-have tool for a crafter who works with a lot of paper. Pulling the paper off of a Cricut cut mat can result in a lot of tearing and paper curling if you are not diligent and mindful when you are removing it. The spatula is thinly designed to slip right under paper which allows you to ease it off the mat carefully. Be sure to clean it often as it is likely to get the adhesive build up on it after multiple uses. It can also be used as a scraper if your scraper tool is not readily available!

Scissors

These sharp tools come in handy more often than you can possibly know with Cricut projects and having a dedicated pair makes it so much easier to complete your projects.

Craft Tweezers

These reverse-action tweezers have a strong grip, precise points, and alleviate cramping after prolonged use.

Spatula

Sometimes you feel like you need an extra set of

hands when you're peeling or laying down a project. This tool gives you that extra support and maneuverability where you need it.

Scoring Stylus

This tool can be loaded into clamp A in your Cricut machine. This will allow the machine to draw deep lines into your project to give it texture or a precise folding point. This same effect can be achieved with other tools on the market, but Cricut makes it simpler and faster with this accessory.

Portable Trimmer

This is a precision cutting tool that allows you to get fast, crisp, straight cuts on your projects 100% of the time. Other versions of this product are available on the market, so keep your eye out for ones with great reviews and a low price point.

Rotary Cutting Kit

This kit includes a gridded cutting mat and a rotary

cutting tool. Cuts are fast, sharp, and precise. This is far from the only rotary tool available on the market, and it's great for cutting fabric and scrapbook pieces.

XL Scraper/Burnishing Tool

This provides a level of control that cannot be beaten. It exerts pressure evenly and helps to eliminate uneven layering and air bubbles. This tool comes very highly recommended by the community of users.

Paper Crafting Set – If you're particularly into papercraft, you will find the edge distresser, quilling tool, piercing tool, and craft mat in this set to be quite to your liking. Quilling or paper filigree art is gaining popularity these days and these are some of the best tools available for that craft.

TrueControl™ Knife

This is a precision blade that is comparable to

XACTO in quality and in type. For more precise freehand cuts, this knife is very helpful at any crafting station.

Cricut Explore® Wireless Bluetooth® Adapter

This product is to help your Cricut Explore machine connect with Bluetooth to your computer or device. The Cricut Maker has this capability built-in, but it can be added to your Explore machine as well.

Deep-Point Replacement Blades

These help your Cricut machine to make more precise cuts with thicker materials!

Bonded Fabric Blades

These blades are meant to retain their extremely sharp point, cut after cut into fabric in your machine!

Replacement Blades

With different purposes like debossing, engraving, perforation and more, can be purchased from Cricut as well. These are specifically for the Cricut Maker model, whereas the replacement blades specified above are for the Cricut Explore models.

The Cricut Easy press

If you begin to venture into iron-on projects and want to upgrade from a traditional iron and ironing board, the Cricut Easy press is the right way to go. It will make projects so much easier than using a traditional iron. The Cricut Easy press is known to help keep designed adhered for longer, essentially no more peeling of designs after one or two uses and washes. The Easy press also takes all of the guesswork out of the right amount of contact time as well as temperature. You will not run the risk of burning your transfer paper or fabric!

The Cricut Brightpad

The lightweight and low profile design of the Cricut

Cricut

Brightpad reduces eyestrain while making crafting easier. It is designed to illuminate fine lines for tracing, cut lines for weeding and so much more! It is thin and lightweight which allows for durable transportation. BrightPad makes crafting more enjoyable with its adjustable, evenly lit surface. The bright LED lights can be adjusted depending on the workspace. The only downfall to this accessory is that it must be plugged in while it is used. It does not contain a rechargeable battery.

The Cricut Cuttlebug Machine

The Cricut Cuttlebug is embossing and dies cutting machine that offers portability and versatility when it comes to cutting and embossing a wide variety of materials. This machine gives professional looking results with clean, crisp, and deep embosses. This machine goes beyond paper, allowing you to emboss tissue paper, foils, thin leather, and more!

CHAPTER 5:

CONFIGURATION OF CRICUT DESIGN SPACE SOFTWARE

How to Install/Uninstall Design Space

There are different platforms that use Cricut Design Space as previously discussed. Let us discuss how to install/uninstall on these platforms including Windows, Mac, iOS and android devices.

Install on Windows/Mac:

- Click on your browser and navigate to **www.design.cricut.com**

- If you are a first time user, you need to create a Cricut ID otherwise sign in with your Cricut ID. Ensure that the page is fully loaded before carrying out this activity in order to avoid error.

- Select New Project.

- Select Download Plugin from the prompt.

- Wait for the download to finish and then select the downloaded file to Open/Run it.

- Click Next when the Cricut installer opens.

- Read the Terms of Use and accept the agreement.

- Click Install to begin installation

- Click Done at the end of the installation.

Install Cricut Design Space App on iOS

- Tap on the App Store icon on your device

- Search for Cricut Design Space

- Tap the Get button to download. Please confirm the download with your iTunes password if prompted. The app will launch and display the necessary options that will used to complete the process.

Install Cricut Design Space App on Android

- Tap Google Play Store App on your device to open it

- Search for Cricut Design Space

- Tap on the Install button

- Tap on the Cricut Design Space icon to open it when the installation is complete

- Sign in and start designing your project

Uninstall the Cricut Design Space on iOS

- Press and hold the Design Space icon on your iOS device till it vibrates

- Press the X button to delete it from your device. This is very easy right?

- Uninstall Cricut Design Space App on Android

- Go to Settings

- Tap on "Apps" or "Applications"

- Swipe to the "Download" tab or "Application Manager"

- Search for the App you intend to uninstall

- Tap "Uninstall" button to finish and the App is gone for good.

Uninstall on Mac

- Move to Finder and open the Applications folder

- Search for Cricut Design Space

- Drag it to trash

- Right click on the Trashcan and select Empty Trash to remove the Application

Uninstall on Windows

- Click on the Start button.

- Select Settings

- Select Application

- Look for Cricut Design Space and choose Uninstall

How to center your designs to cut in Cricut Design Space

- Sign in to the Cricut Design section. Click on the new project.

- Click Download.

- Click Upload Picture.

- Click Browse.

- Save your picture

- Select the saved image and insert an image.

- Select the picture. Click on it.

- As you can see, the picture is automatically

moved to the upper left corner.

- To prevent this, you can fool the software by placing the image in the center of your design area and the mat. This is useful if you want to create openings in the middle of a page.

- Click on the shape tool.

- Create a shape of 11.5 x 11.5 inches.

- Select the square and change the setting to cut it in the drawing.

- The square now appears as an outline.

- Click Align and Center with the selected pattern and square.

- Click the arrow of the size of your square and resize it without moving the top left corner to reduce the size of the square.

- Select the square and pattern, then click Attach. Click on it.

- As you can see now, the design is centered.

How to write with sketch pens in Cricut Design Space

- Sign in to the Cricut Design section. Create a new project.

- Click Download.

- Select upload a picture.

- Click Browse.

- open your file. Then save To get a good effect, use a file with thin lines and no large spaces.

- Click on the pattern and paste it.

- Select the pattern.

- Change the drawing to a drawing.

- You will now see the drawing as an outline drawn.

- Click on it.

- Your drawing will now be displayed on the cutting screen. Click on Continue.

- If you change your drawing to draw, the software automatically selects the pen tool. Insert the pen or marker into the recommended clip. Insert paper and click on the start icon.

- The pen now draws your pattern.

How to upload PNG file in Cricut design space

After you've converted your PDF document to PNG file format, there are some ways to clean up the file before printing and then crop it with Cricut® Design Space.

- Click Create New Project.

- Click Upload Picture.

- Click on the image to upload

- Click Browse

- The Open dialog box opens. Select the PNG file you want to upload and click

- An example of a picture can be found in Cricut® Design Space. Since we want to edit this file, we select Complex Image and click Next

- The PNG file is loaded into Cricut® Design Space. Select and Delete

How to convert a pdf to PNG format

- After downloading the PDF document to your computer, open your browser and go to png2pdf.com.

- Click on the upload files

- The "Open File" dialog box starts. Locate the PDF file to convert (probably in the Downloads folder), click the PDF file and click The file is uploaded. You should see a progress bar. Once the file has been uploaded and converted, a Download button appears below the small image of the uploaded file.

- Click on the download The file is downloaded as a ZIP file and appears in the status bar at the bottom of the screen. Just click on the filename to open the ZIP file.

- The Open File dialog opens, and the downloaded file should be displayed. Since the file is still in ZIP format, you must first unzip or unzip it. Just click Extract All Files.

- The Open File dialog opens, and your newly converted PDF file should be displayed in PNG file. You can open the file with a double-click if you only want to see what the file looks like. Close the window now by clicking on the red X.

- After you have converted your PDF file to PNG format, you must upload the PNG file to Cricut® Design Space so that you can use the

Print and Cut functions.

Working with Edit Bar in Cricut Design Space

Here are important terminologies to help our understanding of the Design Space Edit Bar will have to be defined. A word of caution though, is that some of the terms used here are common tools for everyday use on the computer so it shouldn't be difficult to understand but our level of computer literacy is not the same. Therefore, pardon me if you already know many of them. This has been done for the sake of those who do not know. The terms are as follows:

Undo/Redo- refers to undoing any change made to the layer or redo any previously taken undone action.

Linetype- refers to how the machine will interact with the material on the mat including cut, draw and score as described below.

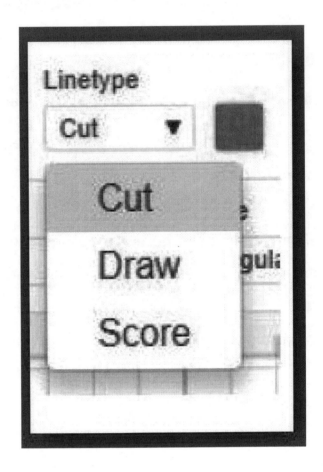

Cut- refers to cutting layer with the aid of a blade from your material.

Draw- refers to drawing the layer with the aid of a Cricut pen.

Score- refers to scoring the layer using a Scoring Stylus or Scoring Wheel.

Linetype Swatch- refers to choosing additional attributes that your layer will use. There are different types of options you can select from based on the selected Linetype (cut, draw, and score).

Working with Fonts in Design Space

The ability to personalize project with the use of distinct fonts and text is one of the unique features of the Cricut Design Space. Why is this unique? Because it gives you the freedom to express the creativity of your mind. This creative ability is innate in us and there is this satisfaction accompanied by a great sense of accomplishment that is felt whenever the projects are delivered to taste.

The Cricut Design Space has another amazing feature which is the ability to change the font after ungrouping or isolating the letters, you can use the Cricut fonts or the one installed on your computer or device.

Cricut

How to Select Font

If you have ever worked with Image Edit Tool before, then you will definitely be at home with the Text Edit tool in Cricut Design Space. This is because the two tools are similar in their mode of operation in rotating, sizing and positioning of text. The similarity of the tools will excite you because it makes the job simpler when editing the text and locating the right font. With this, you can personalize projects easily.

How to Edit Fonts

The Edit bar in Cricut design Space, grants you access to edit the features of particular images or text. These features include Linetype, Size, Rotate, Fill, Position and Mirror. In the Text layers, there are additional options in the Text layers including Line Spacing, font styles and letter spacing. So how do you edit the font? Here, I will show you.

Select the text object you want to edit on the Canvas

or you can insert text from design panel, or select a text layer from the Layers Panel. Once it is selected, the Text Edit Bar will pop up directly below Standard Edit Bar. Note that the Standard Edit Bar will be hidden when you are not interacting with the text.

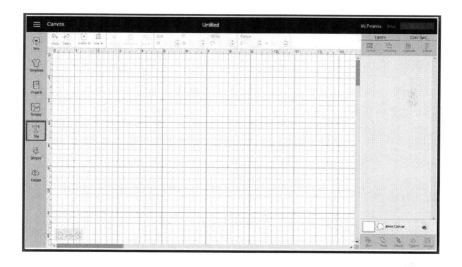

When the Text Edit Bar pops up, you can begin to manipulate the font using the options described below. Simple right?

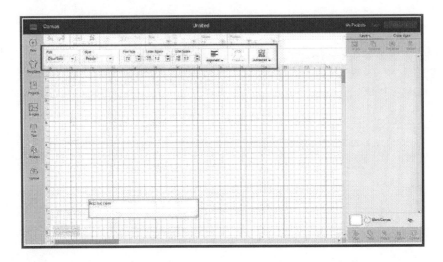

How to Add Text to Cricut Design Space

Navigate to the left hand side of the Canvas and select the ᴛₑₓₜ tool. When the Text tool is selected, the font list will open if you are using iOS/Android or the Text bar and text box will pop up for users with Windows/Mac.

Select the desired font size and the font type you intend to use and then input your text. If you intend to start on a new line of text on the same textbox, use the 'Return' key after the previous line of text. Do not freak out when you did not choose the font setting before typing the text, with Cricut Design

Space, it is possible to type the text before selecting the font on a Windows/Mac computer. Do you remember when this was discussed previously? Of course, you do.

- Click or tap on any area outside the text box to close it.

- To edit the text is pretty simple. Double click on the text to display available options.

- The Edit bar is found at the top of the Canvas fo Windows/Mac users and at the bottom of the Canvas for iOS/Android users.

CHAPTER 6:

HOW TO START YOUR FIRST CUT

So, you have all your materials on hand, which is awesome, but how do you actually **use** a Cricut machine? Well, that's what you're about to find out. If looking at your Cricut machine makes you feel all sorts of confused, then continue reading here, we'll tell you how to use your new Cricut machine in a simple, yet effective manner.

Setting Up the Machine

First, you'll want to set up the Cricut machine. To begin, create a space for it. A craft room is the best place for this, but if you're at a loss of where to put it, I suggest setting it up in a dining room if possible. Make sure you have an outlet nearby or a reliable extension cord.

Next, read the instructions. Often, you can jump right in and begin using the equipment, but with Cricut machines, it can be very tedious. The best thing to do is to read all the materials you get with your machine – while we'll go over the setup in this book, if you're still stumped, take a look at the manual.

Make sure that you do have ample free space around the machine itself, because you will be loading mats in and out and you'll need that little bit of wiggle room.

The next thing to set up is, of course, the computer where the designs will be created. Make sure that whatever medium you're using has an internet connection, since you'll need to download the Cricut Design Space app. If it's a machine earlier than the Explore Air 2, it will need to be plugged in directly, but if it's a wireless machine like the Air 2, you can simply link this up to your computer, and from there, design what you need to design.

Now, once you have the cricut initially set up, you'll want to learn how to use Design Space.

Using Cricut Software

So, Cricut machines use a program called Cricut Design Spaces, and you'll need to make sure that you have this downloaded and installed when you're ready. Download the app if you plan to use a smartphone or tablet, or if you're on the computer, go to http://design.cricut.com/setup to get the software. If it's not hooked up already, make sure you've got Bluetooth compatibility enabled on the device, or the cord plugged in. To turn on your machine, hold the power button. You'll then go to settings, where you should see your Cricut model in Bluetooth settings. Choose that, and from there, your device will ask you to put a Bluetooth passcode in. Just make this something generic and easy to remember.

Once that's done, you can now use Design Space.

When you're in the online mode, you'll see a lot of projects that you can use. For the purpose of this tutorial, I do suggest making sure that you choose an easy one, such as the "Enjoy Card" project you can get automatically.

So, you've got everything all linked up – let's move onto the first cut for this project.

Imputing Cartridges and Keypad

The first cut that you'll be doing does involve keypad input and cartridges, and these are usually done with the "Enjoy Card" project you get right away. So, once everything is set up, choose this project, and from there, you can use the tools and the accessories within the project.

You will need to set the smart dial before you get started making your projects. This is on the right side of the Explore Air 2, and it's basically the way you choose your materials. Turn the dial to whatever type of material you want, since this does help with ensuring you've got the right blade settings. There are even half settings for those in-between projects.

For example, let's say you have some light cardstock. You can choose that setting, or the adjacent half setting. Once this is chosen in Design Space, your machine will automatically adjust to the correct setting.

You can also choose the fast mode, which is in the "set, load, go" area on the screen, and you can then check the position of the box under the indicator for dial position. Then, press this and make your cut. However, fast mode is incredibly loud, so be careful.

Now, we've mentioned cartridges. While these usually aren't used in the Explore Air 2 machines anymore, they are helpful with beginner projects. To do this, once you have the Design Space software and everything is connected, go to the hamburger menu and you'll see an option called "ink cartridges." Press that cricut, and from there, choose the Cricut device. The machine will then tell you to put your cartridge in. Do that, and once it's detected, it will tell you to link the cartridge.

Do remember, though, that once you link this, you can't use it with other machines – the one limit to these cartridges.

Once it's confirmed, you can go to images, and click the cartridges option to find the ones that you want to make. You can filter the cartridges to figure out what you need, and you can check out your images tab for any other cartridges that are purchased or uploaded.

You can get digital cartridges, which means you buy them online and choose the images directly from your available options. They aren't physical, so there is no linking required.

Loading and Unloading Your Paper

To load paper into a Cricut machine, you'll want to make sure that the paper is at least three inches by three inches. Otherwise, it won't cut very well. You should use regular paper for this.

Now, to make this work, you need to put the paper onto the cutting mat. You should have one of those, so take it right now and remove the attached film. Put a corner of the paper to the area where you are directed to align the paper corners. From there, push the paper directly onto the cutting mat for proper adherence. Once you do that, you just load it into the machine, following the arrows. You'll want to keep the paper firmly on the mat. Press the "load paper" key that you see as you do this. If it doesn't take for some reason, press the unload paper key, and try this again until it shows up.

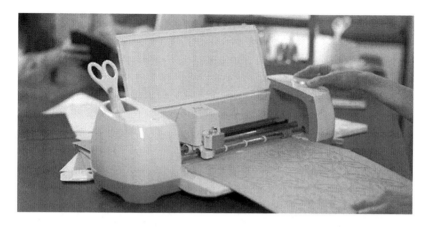

Now, before you do any cutting for your design, you should always have a test cut in place. Some people don't do this, but it's incredibly helpful when learning how to use a Cricut. Otherwise, you won't get the pressure correct in some cases, so get in the habit of doing it for your pieces.

Selecting Shapes, Letters, And Phrases

When you're creating your design in Design Space, you usually begin by using letters, shapes, numbers, or different fonts. These are the basics, and they're incredibly easy.

To make text, you just press the text tool on the left-hand side and type out your text. For example, write the word hello, or joy, or whatever you want to use.

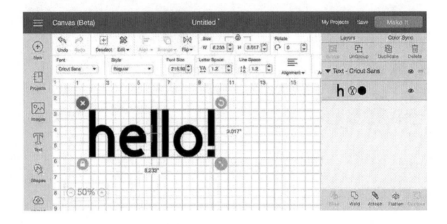

You can choose different Cricut or system fonts, too. Cricut ones will be in green, and if you have Cricut Access, this is a great way to begin using this. You can sort these, too, so you don't end up accidentally paying for a font.

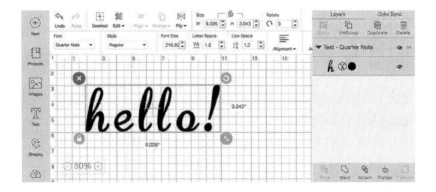

The Cricut ones are supposed to be made for Cricut, so you know they'll look good. Design Space also lets you put them closer together so they can be cut with a singular cut. You can change this by going to line spacing and adjusting as needed. To fix certain letters, you go to the drop-down advanced menu to ungroup the letters, so everything is separate as needed.

Cricut also offers different writing styles, which is a great way to add text to projects. The way to do this is to choose a font that's made with a specific style and choose only the Cricut ones, and then go to writing. This will then narrow down the choice so you're using a good font for writing.

Adding shapes is pretty easy, as well. In Design Space, choose the shapes option. Once you click it, the window will then pop out, and you'll have a wonderful array of different shapes that you can use with just one click. Choose your shape, and from there, put it in the space. Drag the corners in order

Cricut

to make this bigger or smaller.

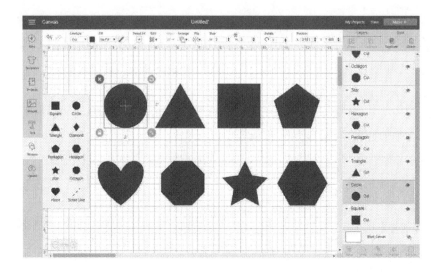

There is also the score line, which creates a folding line for you to use. Personally, if you're thinking of trying to make a card at first, I suggest using this.

You can also resize your options by dragging them towards the right-hand side, and you can change the orientation by choosing that option, and then flipping it around. You can select exact measurements as well, which is good for those design projects that need everything to be precise.

Once you've chosen the design, it's time for you to

start cutting.

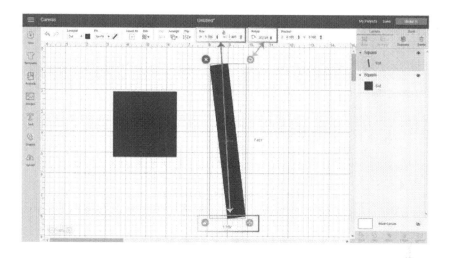

How to Remove Your Cut from The Cutting Mat?

Removing your cut from the mat is easy, but complicated. Personally, I ran into the issue of it being more complicated with vinyl projects since they love to just stick around there. But we'll explain how you can create great cuts and remove them, as well.

The first thing to remember is to make sure that you're using the right mat. The light grip ones are good for very light material, with the pink one being one of the strongest, and only to be used with the Cricut Maker. Once the design is cut, you'll probably be eager about removing the project directly from the mat, but one of the problems with this is that often, the project will be ruined if you're not careful. Instead of pulling the project from the mat itself, bend the mat within your hand, and push it away from the project, since this will loosen it from the mat. Bend this both horizontally and vertically, so that the adhesive releases the project.

Use this spatula to lightly pull on the vinyl, until you can grab it from the corner and lift it up. Otherwise, you risk curling it or tearing the mat, which is what we don't want.

Now, with the initial cuts, such as the paper ones,

this will be incredibly easy. Trust me, I was surprised at how little effort it took, but one of the biggest things to remember is that with Cricut machines, you have to go slow when removing the material. Do this slowly, and don't get rushed near the end. Taking your time will save you a lot of problems, and it will even save you money and stress, too!

You will notice that Cricut mats are incredibly sticky, and if you don't have a Cricut spatula on hand or don't want to spend the money, metal spatulas will work, too. You can put the paper on a flat surface and then lightly remove it. But always be careful when removing these items.

Cricut machines are pretty easy to use, and the beauty is that with the right understanding and ideas, you can make any items you want to.

CHAPTER 7:

COMMON LIST OF PROBLEMS WITH CRICUT MACHINE AND HOW TO SOLVE THEM

Material Tearing or Not Cutting Completely Through

This is the biggest problem with most Cricut users. When this happens, the image is ruined, and you've wasted material. More machines have been returned or boxed up and put away due to this problem than any other.

But don't panic, if your paper is not cutting correctly there are several steps you can take to try and correct the problem.

Most important is this: Anytime you work with the blade TURN YOUR MACHINE OFF. I know it's easy to forget this because you're frustrated and you're trying this and that to make it work correctly. But this is an important safety precaution that you should remember.

Make simple adjustments at first. Turn the pressure down one. Did it help? If not, turn the blade down one number. Also, make sure the mat is free of debris so the blade rides smoothly.

Usually the thicker the material, the higher the pressure number should be set to cut through the paper. Don't forget to use the **multi cut function** if you have that option. It may take a little longer to cut 2, 3 or 4 times, but by then it should cut clean through.

For those of you using the smaller bugs that do not have that option here is how to **make your own multi-cut function**. After the image has been cut, don't unload the mat just hit load paper, repeat last and cut. You can repeat this sequence 2, 3 or 4 times to ensure your image is completely cut out.

If you are using thinner paper and it is tearing try reducing the pressure and slowing down the speed. When cutting intricate designs, you have to give the blade enough time to maneuver through the design. By slowing it down it will be able to make cleaner cuts.

Clean the edge of the blade to be sure no fuzz, glue or scraps of paper are stuck to it.

Make sure the blade is installed correctly. Take it out and put it back so it's seated firmly. The blade should be steady while it's making cuts. If it makes a shaky movement it's either not installed correctly, or there's a problem with the **blade housing**.

Be aware that there is a deep cutting blade for thicker material. You'll want to switch to this blade when you're cutting heavy card stock. This will also save wear and tear on your regular blade. Cutting a lot of thick material will obviously wear your blade out quicker than thinner material and cause you to change it more often.

Machine Freezing

Remember to always turn your machine off when you switch cartridges. When you switch cartridges leaving the machine on it's called "hot swapping" and it can sometimes cause the machine to freeze. This is more of an issue with the older models and doesn't seem to apply to the Expression 2.

You know how quirky electronic gadgets can be, so give your machine a rest for five or ten minutes every hour. If you work for several hours continuously, your machine might overheat and freeze up.

Turn the machine off and take a break. Restart it when you come back and it should be fine. Then remember not to rush programming the machine and give it an occasional rest.

Don't press a long list of commands quickly. If you

give it too much information too quickly it will get confused in the same way a computer sometimes does and simply freeze up. Instead of typing in one long phrase try dividing up your **words into several cuts**.

If you're using **special feature keys** make sure you press them first before selecting the letters.

Power Problems

If you turn your machine on and nothing happens the power adapter may be at fault. Jiggle the power cord at the outlet and where it connects to the machine to make sure it's firmly connected. Ideally, you want to test the adapter before buying a new one. Swap cords with a friend and see if that fixed the problem. Replacement adapters can be found on eBay by searching for Cricut adapter power supply.

The **connection points** inside the machine may also pose a problem; here is how to test that. Hold down the plug where it inserts into the back of the machine and turn it on. If it powers up, then the problem is inside the machine and the connection points will have to be soldered again.

If the machine powers up but will not cut then try a hard reset. See the resource section for step-by-step instructions on resetting your machine.

Here are a few tips especially for Expression 2 users. Have you turned on your machine, you watch it light up and hear it gearing up but when you try to cut nothing happens? Or you're stuck on the welcome screen or the LCD screen is unresponsive.

Well here are two quick fixes to try. First try a hard reset sometimes called the **rainbow screen reset** to recalibrate your die cutter. If that does not resolve the problem you're going to have to restore the settings.

To help cut down on errors try to keep your machine updated. When an update is available, you should receive a message encouraging you to install the latest version.

For those of you using third party software that is no longer compatible with the Cricut you probably already know that **updating your machine may disable that software**.

When you cut heavy paper and your Expression 2 shuts down try switching to the normal paper setting and use the **multi cut function**.

Carriage Will Not Move

If the carriage assembly does not move, check to see if the **belt has broken or if the car has fallen off the track**. Provo Craft does not sell replacement parts, which is nuts, so try to find a compatible belt at a vacuum repair shop.

If the wheels have fallen off the track, remove the plastic cover and look for a tiny screw by the wheel unscrew it. You now should be able to move the wheel back on track.

Unresponsive Keyboard

If you are sure you are pressing the keys firmly, you have a cartridge inserted correctly and a mat loaded ready to go, but the keypad is still not accepting your selection, the problem may be internal.

You will have to remove the keyboard and check if the **display cable is connected to the keypad and to the motherboard**. If the connections are secure then you have a circuit board problem and repairs are beyond the scope of this book.

An important reminder, please do not attempt any repairs unless your machine is out of warranty.

Weird LCD Screen

The LCD screen is now showing strange symbols or is blank after doing a firmware update. Try running the update again making sure your selections are correct.

When the image you choose is bigger than the mat

or paper size you selected the preview screen will look **grayed out** instead of showing the image. So increase the paper and mat size or decrease the size of your image.

Also watch out for the gray box effect when using the **center point feature**. Move the start position down until you see the image appear. The same thing may happen when using the fit to length feature. Try changing to landscape mode and shorten the length size until the image appears.

Occasionally using the **undo button** will cause the preview screen to turn black; unfortunately the only thing to do is turn the machine off. Your work will be lost and you have to start again.

Cartridge Errors

Sometimes dust or debris accumulates in the cartridge port gently blow out any paper fiber that may have collected in the opening. Make sure the contact points are clean and that nothing is preventing the cartridge from being read properly.

With any electrical machine overheating can be a problem. If you get a cartridge error after using your machine for a while turn it off and let it cool down for about fifteen minutes.

If this is the very first time you're using the cartridge and you get an error I'm sure you know the trick about turning the cartridge around and inserting it in backward.

If you thought you could use your Imagine cartridges with your Expression 2, think again. You will get an error message because you can only use the **art cartridges** that you can cut with, the colors and patterns cartridge are for printing.

Even brand-new items fresh out of the box can be defective. If you see a cartridge error 1, 2, 3, 4, 5, 6, 9 or 99 call customer service and tell them the name, serial number and error message number and they may replace the cartridge.

Trouble Connecting to Your Computer

All Cricut machines come with a USB cord that lets you connect to your computer and allows you to use the other products like the Cricut Design Studio software, Cricut Craft Room or the Cricut Gypsy with your machines.

Double check your USB connection and try another port.

Check to see if you may have a firewall or antivirus software that is blocking the connection.

See if you're running the latest firmware. You may need to update. Older machines update via firmware (Personal Cutter, Expression, Create and Cake) the newer (Expression 2, Imagine and Gypsy) use the Sync program to update.

CHAPTER 8:

MAINTAINING THE CRICUT

Every Cricut machine needs to be cleaned and taken care of in order to keep it working for as long as possible. Here, you'll learn about the maintenance required for Cricut machines, and what you can do to keep your machine working efficiently.

Cleaning and Care

Cleaning your machine is very important, and you should do it regularly to keep everything in tip-top shape. If you don't take care of your machine, that's just money down the drain.

But what can you do to care for your machine? Well, I do suggest initially that you make sure to run maintenance on it as much as you can and keep it clean. There are a few other tips and tricks that can help prolong the machine's life. For starters, keep liquids and food away from the machine – never drink or eat while you use your Cricut machine. Set up your machine in a location that's free of dust and try to keep it away from excessive coolness or heat, so don't just throw it in the attic or an especially cold basement. If you're transporting your machine to use it at a different location, never leave it in the car. Excessive heat will melt the machine's plastic components, so be careful.

Finally, make sure the machine is stored away from sunlight. Keep it out of places in the home where sunlight hits it directly. For example, if you have an office that is very bright and the sun warms the machine for a long period of time, you'll want to move it so that it doesn't get damaged.

Be gentle with your machine. Remember, it is a machine, so you'll want to make sure that you do take some time and try to keep it nice and in order. Don't be rough with it, and when working with the machine parts, don't be too rough with them, either.

Caring for your machine isn't just about making sure that the parts don't get dirty, but you should also make sure that you keep everything in good working order.

Ensure your machine is on stable footing.

This may seem pretty basic, but ensuring that your machine is on a level surface will allow it to make more precise cuts every single time. Rocking of the machine or wobbling could cause unstable results in your projects.

Ensure no debris has gotten stuck under the feet of your machine that could cause instability before proceeding to the next troubleshooting step!

Redo all Cable Connections

So your connections are in the best possible working order, undo all your cable connection, blow into the ports or use canned air, and then securely plug everything back into the right ports. This will help to make sure all the connections are talking to each other where they should be!

Completely Dust and Clean Your Machine

Your little Cricut works hard for you! Return the favor by making sure you're not allowing gunk, dust, grime, or debris to build up in the surfaces and crevices. Adhesive can build up on the machine around the mat input and on the rollers, so be sure to focus on those areas!

Check Your Blade Housing

Sometimes debris and leavings from your materials can build up inside the housings for your blades! Open them up and clear any built-up materials that could be impeding swiveling or motion.

Sharpen Your Blades

A very popular Cricut trick in use is to stick a clean, fresh piece of foil to your cricut mat, and run it through with the blade you wish to sharpen. Running the blades through the thin metal helps to revitalize their edges and give them a little extra staying power until it's time to buy replacements.

Cleaning the Machine Itself

In general, the exterior is pretty easy to clean – you just need a damp cloth. Use a soft cloth to wipe it off, and keep in mind that chemical cleaners with benzene, acetone, or carbon tetrachloride should never be used on your Cricut machine. Any cleaner that is scratchy, as well, should be avoided at all costs.

Make sure that you never put any machine components in water. This should be obvious, but often, people may use a piece of a damp cloth, thinking that it'll be fine when in reality, it isn't.

You should consider getting some non-alcoholic wipes for cleaning your machine. Always disconnect the power before cleaning, as you would with any machine. The Cricut machine can then be lightly wiped down. Some people also use a glass cleaner sprayed on a cloth but do be careful to make sure no residue builds up. If you notice there is some dust there, you can typically get away with a cloth that's soft and clean.

Sometimes, grease can build up – you may notice this on the cartridge bar if you use cartridges a lot. Use a swab of cotton or a soft cloth to remove it.

Greasing the Machine

If you need to grease your machine, first make sure that it's turned off and the smart carriage is moved to the left. Use a tissue to wipe this down, and then move it to the right, repeating the process again.

From there, move the carriage to the center and open up a lubrication package. Put a small amount onto a Q-tip. Apply a thin coating, greasing everything evenly, and also clean any buildup that may have occurred. This is usually the issue if you hear grinding noise when cleaning the machine itself.

Never use spray cleaner directly on the machine, for obvious reasons. The bar holding the housing shouldn't be wiped down, but if you do notice an excessive grease, please take the time to make sure that it's cleaned up. Remember to never touch the gear chain near the back of this unit, either, and never clean with the machine on, for your own safety.

Cricut machines are great, but you need to take care in making sure that you keep everything in rightful order.

Cutting Blade

Your blades will tend to dull over time, but this is usually a very slow process. The best way to prevent it is to have different blades to cut different materials. Having a different blade for each material is a really good idea.

You can get fine-point ones which are good for smaller items; deep-cut, which is great for leather and other fabrics; bonded fabric, so great for fabric pieces; a rotary blade for those heavy fabrics; and finally, a knife blade, which is good for those really thick items.

In order to maintain your blades, you should clean the housing area for every blade after each use, since they get gunky fast. Squirting compressed air into the area is a wonderful way to get the dust out of there.

Cutting Mat

Your cutting mats need to be cleaned because if you don't clean them frequently, they will attract dirt and lose adhesiveness. That means you'll have to spend more money on mats, which isn't ideal. There are different ways to clean them, and we'll go over a few of the different means to clean your mats so you can use them for longer.

Cleaning the Mat Itself

First, if your mat is completely filthy, you need to clean it. Of course, you'll also want to do this for just general maintenance, too. Once it's been cleaned, you'll notice it's sticky again.

Typically, washing it down with either a magic eraser or a kitchen scrubber can do it. Sometimes, if it's really dirty, you might want to get some rubbing alcohol onto a wipe. If you notice a chunk of the debris left behind, however, is fabric oriented, then get some lint rollers or even just stick some scotch tape on there and pull it off. This can eliminate the issue.

CHAPTER 9:

HOW TO MAKE MONEY WITH CRICUT MACHINE

Just as the Cricut machine can be used in a million and one ways, the ways to generate money from it is also numerous.

Some of the ways to generate money from the Cricut machine are highlighted below:

Make and Sell Leather Bracelets

Bracelets are fashionable items, especially leather bracelet. The Cricut machine can easily cut real or faux leather easily giving you less work to do. You decide to cut, make, and sell leather bracelets, considering the materials needed are just snaps, your Cricut machine, leather, and probably card stock.

If you are interested in selling this craft, you can also create room for preordering, where a buyer can order for a particular design to be created by the designer.

Sell Iron-On Vinyl

This is another money-making opportunity that the Cricut machine provides. You make a design with the iron-on vinyl and sell out to people. The iron-on vinyl can be in the form of text or design. It can also be made for each season or celebration, be it Valentine, Halloween, Christmas, or Easter. Buyers may also order for what they want.

Sell Stickers

This idea is targeted at kids. You can make money by designing educative and entertaining stickers for toddlers and other age groups. Stickers of alphabet or map of a locale can be made. Stickers are also used in decorating places like the wardrobe or closets.

Make and Sell Party Decorations and Buntings

There is always a celebration in our day-to-day lives as human beings. It can be a milestone celebration or simply a fun-seeking escapade. Party decorations made with the Cricut machine can be sold at these occasions.

Window decals

Everyone has a peculiar image, an object we are practically obsessed with. Getting a vinyl window decal of one's favorite image will go a long way in giving your decor a boost. Making and selling window decal is quite easy and profitable.

Make and sell canvas wall art

Customized wall art would generate quick and easy money. Get inspirational sayings or design and make them into wall arts for sale.

Design and sell onesies

Onesies or bodysuit are generally cute cloth which can be better with amazing artwork. Onesies for babies can be made with a lot of other text apart from "Daddy loves you" or "Momma's baby." Other mushy word art can be used in designing onesies for kids.

Become a Cricut affiliate

This entails being paid to make tutorials video by the Cricut company. These videos are uploaded to the internet for the netizen to make use of. To become a Cricut affiliate, you need to have a strong internet presence. You must also have a tangible amount of followers on his or her social media accounts.

Post tutorial videos on your vlog

This has nothing to do with being an affiliate; rather, you create a blog for videos and upload tutorial videos and get paid through the generated traffic.

Use of social media

You can make any of the craft you find easy and post pictures of it online, announcing to those on your list that it is for sale. This works better because whoever is buying get to see the picture of whatever he is getting before ordering for it. Personalized crafts should also be included in your order of business.

Design and sell T-shirts

T-shirt is a clothing piece that is always in vogue. Most especially for college students, a designed tee would be a great fashion item. Creating a designed T-shirt would generate income.

Design and sell hoodies

Hoodies are great wears for cold seasons. A designed one would roll better with the youth. The design can be preordered too.

Design and sell leather neck piece

Aleather pendant can be designed for a necklace and sold out to interested buyers. An all leather neck piece can also be made and sold.

Design and sell banners

Banners can be made for celebration, festive periods, camping, parties, religious activities, or sporting activities. All these can be made and sold.

Design and sell window clings

Window clings with the design of the seasons can be made and sold. Other designs or image can also be used for creating window clings.

Design and sell stencils

Stencils can be created and sold for those that want to hand-paint a post or sign. It would also generate a nice amount of money.

Design and sell safari animal stickers

Stickers of safari animals are attractive items. They can be and sold to animal lovers. The sticker is easy to make and will also be a source of income generation.

Design and sell labeling stickers

Labeling stickers can be made for labeling things in the house. Things in the kitchen, pantry, playroom, classroom, and other places can be labeled with labeling stickers.

Design and sell Christmas ornaments

Christmas is a period people celebrate and decorate their workplace, abode, and religious settings, among others.

Design and sell doormats

Beautiful doormat can be made with the machine and sold to customers. It can be designed with either text or images. Customized doormats can also be sold.

Design and sell kitchen towels

Towels used in the kitchen can be designed and sold at affordable prices. The towels can be designed with text or images of delicacies.

There are countless things you can make with Cricut. Likewise, there are countless things you can make, which are marketable. Independent entrepreneurship is easier than it's ever been thanks to the internet and web platforms that make selling your products a breeze.

You've likely already heard of some of the platforms that make it easy to start a shop of your own. Etsy is probably the most well-known of these platforms and setting up a shop with them is so simple, it's almost impossible not to be interested in starting one for yourself!

With the Cricut, making countless items of every type and theme, for any and all occasions, is the name of the game. Doing these projects can be a huge source of joy for the avid crafter, but if you're spending the money on the materials for your projects, it might make sense for you to start generating a return on those, depending on how much you're doing and spending.

What are the Best Platforms on Which to sell my Crafts?

This question is a little bit loaded and, what it boils down to is which platform is the most convenient, workable, and reliable for you. The business you want to create is going to take up a lot of your time and attention, so it's imperative that you're using a platform that fits all your needs, meets all your expectations, and solves more problems for you than it causes.

We can tend to be forgiving of quirks in new systems when we're learning them. However, take a little extra time to read the experiences and reviews of people who have used that platform for an extended period of time. This will give you a look

117

into what your future could be like with that platform, and it's the only gauge you have to go by when it comes to how that platform will serve you.

You will want to spend a little extra time looking into which platforms are available, what costs are involved (if any), how they treat their sellers, what percentages of your sales are taken, and what the sellers on those platforms think of them.

Here are some of the top platforms you'll want to check into!

- Etsy
- Amazon Handmade
- Facebook Marketplace
- Folksy
- Artfire
- Craftsy
- eBay
- Craigslist

CHAPTER 10:

TIPS AND TRICKS

Organize your tools and label your buttons.

If you are able to you can subscribe to the access for about ten dollars a month to gain access to over twenty thousand different images and over a thousand different projects. You even get over three hundred fonts.

If you have an Air 2 the mat can be sticky. Peel off your cover and then place a dry shirt over the mat (make sure that it is clean) to prime it for your first project. What this does is it helps with that stickiness from the card stock without damaging your first project.

Set your dial as this is important. Turn it to the correct material setting. If you don't it can ruin the cuts your making because it's on the wrong one.

If you have a small design or something that's more intricate then you can use what is known as a weeding box, this is also a good idea when your cutting on one mat for multiple designs.

When you are cutting vinyl that is heat transfer you will need to remember to mirror the design.

When you are using vinyl you also need to remember that you need to place your vinyl right way up on your mat for cutting. For heat transfer place its shiny side down.

When beginning to understand the correct use of your cutting mat then you need to make sure that you are loading you mat correctly so that both sides are sliding under the rollers. If you don't do this it won't load properly.

You will also need to keep the plastic sheets that come with the mats to protect them between your uses.

Clean your cutting mats with baby wipes that are water-based to keep them sticky and clean longer.

Use one blade for your cardstock and a separate one for vinyl because this will let them both last longer.

Make sure that you have a deep cut blade.

This is going to allow you to cut through thicker materials like chipboard or leather. The blade would be compatible with the Air 2. Remember we said the Maker cuts deeper, but the others can't. This blade will help but remember to order your housing for the blade as well.

This is for people who have had the cartridges for an older machine or older cartridge. You can hook these up to your new account. It is a simple thing to do but you should know that you could only link them once so be sure that if you are buying a machine second hand that nothing has been linked yet.

This is probably going to seem like a no brainer but it's actually a serious tip that you will need to remember. Remember not to leave your pen in the machine after you've completed a project. You get so involved in what you're doing that you can forget about the supplies and the things of that nature that you leave in it there but guess what? The next time you reach for it, it will be dried out and you can't use it. Replace the cap and make sure it's not drying out. They can be expensive, and you don't want to waste them. Most projects are encouraging this tip as well because it is so important.

The right tools are important here so you should make sure that you have the toolset. It will contain vital tools that you need, and they can especially help with vinyl.

Know your glue

Many people are huge fans of what is called tacky glue. It gives your projects a little bit of wiggle room when you're trying to position them. The problem is that it can take longer to dry. If this is something that bothers you, you might want to try a quicker one. Zip dry paper glue it's extremely sticky and much faster.

A tip that will go along with the tip above is that if you want them to be a layer to pop out from another layer. You can make this happen by using products like pop dots or Zots. They are foam mounts that are self-adhesive. You can also make little circles by using craft foam or cardboard and then glue it between the layers.

You don't have to get your materials from a craft store. In all honesty, they can be quite expensive. There are ways around this (coupons, sales things like that), however, you can shop online or local sign shops. Some even offer you scraps for free in some cases. If there is something that you need such as cardstock, then you should print out the color you need and then cut it out so that you can bring it with you.

Profound Knowledge

The crude materials of configuration may be documentation, a perfect workbench, studio, easels, paints, ability, and information. A performer has to know scales. A painter needs to get tones. A stone carver needs a sharp eye for negative space. An essayist must have a feeling of style.

Figure out how to trust and pursue your impulses

In the event that you ask any effective businessman what has prompted their prosperity, they once in a while state it? They for the most part say one essential key to business achievement is trusting and following your impulses. Achievement can emerge out of basically acting naturally.

Think about a Coach

Business mentors are extremely popular nowadays. Consider going through some cash with a

Scrapbooking business mentor who comprehends the business as well as genuinely comprehends the specific brand of energy scrapbook sweethearts share. A mentor can help share business abilities however can go about as an extraordinary coach in managing you to your objectives.

Exhibit Your True Talent With a Business Card for Artists

The financial downturn has left huge numbers of us feeling the squeeze. Numerous individuals are searching for approaches to set aside cash in each part of life. Be that as it may, there are times when a buy must be made, and cautious research regularly structures some portion of the basic leadership the procedure.

Give the Quality of Your Work A chance to radiate Through

A business card for specialists is your window to the world, and it should say a great deal regarding your aesthetic edge and abilities. Make it state every little thing about you and what you can offer. Plan a motivating logo that can join the substance of what you can do with an incredible structure. This astute connecting can put you on top of things by helping individuals to recollect who and what you are.

Consider Other Ways You Can Display Your Skills to the World

A business card for specialists is only one of numerous limited time apparatuses you can use to enhance your presentation. It bodes well. The production of a notice is a magnificent method to demonstrate the best of what you do. Try not to place a lot into your sign; that will go about as an obstacle and prevent individuals from getting a vibe of your actual abilities. Consider the area where you can show your blurb. Vital arranging of the setting of your sign can help augment its effect. It will expand the intrigue of your work and open up more potential outcomes.

Remember to tell individuals how to connect!

A business card for specialists needs not exclusively to demonstrate the embodiment of your innovativeness; it likewise fills a need. It needs to tell potential clients how to connect with you. Incorporate all the distinctive contact techniques you have, email, site, telephone numbers, and any online networking you are an individual from. Remember about the intensity of internet based life and bookmarking destinations; they can enable feature to considerably a greater amount of your work.

Be Adaptable

Consider chipping away at zones that you hadn't imagined, however will be something inside your abilities. This will enable you to set up a notoriety. Another viable method to advance your aptitudes notwithstanding utilizing a business card for specialists is to engage in network ventures where you offer your administrations for nothing. Make something stunning that individuals will see every day; this is an incredible advert for your aptitudes. This will place your work into the lives of thousands of individuals and will drive more clients to you.

CONCLUSION

This guide has taken you to a new horizon where your creativity will know no bounds using this amazing machine. I hope this book has helped you master the Cricut Design Space. It's a great little machine that can do so many different operations and allows you to make designs for inside and outside your home, to keep, to sell, and to give as gifts.

Cricut may seem complicated at first, but there is a lot you can do with this machine – and a lot that you can get out of it. If you feel confused by Cricut, then take your time, get familiar with the buttons, and start having fun with it.

With Cricut, anything is possible. If you've been wondering what you can do with your machine, the simple answer is almost anything. For designers, for those who like to make precise cuts, and for those who like to print their own shirts, this is a wonderful option to consider. If you are thinking of getting a Cricut machine, you'll see here that there is a lot that you can do with this unique tool, and endless creative possibilities.

The next step is simple – if you have a Cricut machine, get familiar with it. Learn more about it and see for yourself some of the fun things you can do with Cricut, and the cool basic projects you can try now.

It can help you make a lot of handmade things which not only save you money but your time as well blessing you with beautiful products that you can use for yourself as well as the gift to others. You can make handmade cards, design your t-shirt, create your ornaments, and design an envelope and many more.

If you have yet to purchase your first machine, I hope this helps your decision. We want you to enjoy Cricut Design Space and much as thousands of users around the world.

Keep the tips and tricks provided close by as a reference guide so you aren't searching all over to find the answers to your questions.

Never stop doing research. Never stop trying new things. Never, ever stop being creative. The Cricut does not make you any less creative; it just makes the process easier so that you can focus your valuable time and efforts on more important things or personalizing the projects after making the cuts. It takes the tedious work out of your hands and makes everything fun, easy, and fast.

Cricut

Made in the USA
Columbia, SC
30 November 2023

27469572R00074